ROCKS AND MINERALS

IGNEOUS
ROCKS

by Lisa Owings

Content Consultant
Alan Boudreau
Earth and Ocean Sciences
Duke University

Core Library

An Imprint of Abdo Publishing
www.abdopublishing.com

www.abdopublishing.com

Published by Abdo Publishing, a division of ABDO, PO Box 398166, Minneapolis, Minnesota 55439. Copyright © 2015 by Abdo Consulting Group, Inc. International copyrights reserved in all countries. No part of this book may be reproduced in any form without written permission from the publisher. Core Library™ is a trademark and logo of Abdo Publishing.

Printed in the United States of America, North Mankato, Minnesota
042014
092014

 THIS BOOK CONTAINS RECYCLED MATERIALS

Cover Photo: Pecold/Shutterstock Images
Interior Photos: Pecold/Shutterstock Images, 1; Thinkstock, 4, 14, 18, 25, 30, 32, 39; EJ-J/Thinkstock, 6; Shutterstock Images, 10, 29; Banana Republic Images/Shutterstock Images, 12; George W. Bailey/Shutterstock Images, 17; Artography/Shutterstock Images, 22, 45; Alexander Maksimov/Thinkstock, 27; Ted S. Warren/AP Images, 35; Jeff Coe/US Geological Survey, 37; Fuse/Thinkstock, 42 (top); Julien Grondin/Thinkstock, 42 (bottom); Vitaly Raduntsev/Thinkstock, 43

Editor: Jenna Gleisner
Series Designer: Becky Daum

Library of Congress Control Number: 2014932348

Cataloging-in-Publication Data
Owings, Lisa.
 Igneous rocks / Lisa Owings.
   p. cm. -- (Rocks and minerals)
Includes bibliographical references and index.
ISBN 978-1-62403-387-2
1. Igneous rocks--Juvenile literature.   I. Title.
552/.1--dc23
                                                        2014932348

CONTENTS

CHAPTER ONE

THE LIFE CYCLE OF IGNEOUS ROCKS

H ave you ever found an arrowhead in a field or along a stream? If it was glassy and dark, it was probably made of a rock called obsidian. Maybe you have admired granite on the front of a fancy building. Have you ever used a stone to smooth out the rough spots on the bottoms of your feet? It was probably pumice. All of these rocks are igneous

Igneous rocks can form from the lava that erupts from a volcano and cools.

Your kitchen countertops might be made of a polished igneous rock called granite.

rocks. Igneous rocks form when molten, or melted, rock cools.

Rocks are made up of different combinations of minerals. Some common minerals you may know about are salt and gold. Minerals, or crystals, are hard substances that can form underground or on Earth's surface. Next time you see a rock, pick it up. Look closely at it. Can you see different colors or textures? You are looking at the rock's own special combination of minerals.

Three Major Types of Rock

There are three major types of rock on Earth. Sedimentary rocks are made up of small rock particles that were carried by water or wind. Over time, the particles formed layers, with the newer layers on top packing down the older layers on the bottom into rock. Metamorphic rocks are old rocks that were changed into new rocks by heat and pressure. Igneous rocks tell the story of Earth's earliest days. They were the first rocks to grace the surface of our planet. Today igneous rocks are thought to make up approximately 95 percent of Earth's crust.

Layers of Earth

To understand more about how igneous rocks form, we have to find out what goes on inside the earth. Underneath all of Earth's forests, fields, and oceans is a layer of rock. This outer rock layer is called the crust. It feels thick and solid. But compared to the rest of the earth, the crust is as thin as an eggshell. It is cracked in places, forming several large pieces called

Tectonic Plates and Igneous Rock

Tectonic plates can move toward or away from each other. They can also slide past each other. When plates move away from each other, magma wells up to fill in the gap. It cools to form a new crust of igneous rock. When plates move toward each other, one plate gets shoved under the other. As the lower plate is pushed deeper into the mantle, the rock melts, forming magma. The magma causes volcanoes and forms new igneous rock. Igneous rock is not often formed when plates slide past each other. But this movement often causes severe earthquakes.

tectonic plates. The plates move slowly. They cause earthquakes or volcanoes when they crash into or rub against one another. Most new igneous rock forms along the edges of tectonic plates.

The layer beneath the crust is the mantle. If the crust is like an eggshell, the mantle is like the egg white. The upper part of the mantle is solid rock. But the deeper into the earth you go, the hotter it gets. In the lower part of the mantle, temperatures rise so high that rocks begin to melt. The hottest place on Earth is its innermost layer, called the core. The core is like the egg yolk. It is made of metal. Its outer part is liquid, and its inner part is solid.

The journey of an igneous rock begins deep inside the earth's mantle. There, rock sometimes gets hot enough to melt into a liquid called magma. The fiery magma tries to rise toward Earth's surface. It seeps into cracks and weak places in the rock above. It also wells up between tectonic plates. As the magma rises, it cools. As it cools, it becomes solid. And that is how new igneous rocks are formed.

Earth's Core

Earth's core is approximately the size of Mars. But it is buried so deep inside the earth that no human has ever explored it. Temperatures in the earth's core can rise up to 12,100 degrees Fahrenheit (6,700°C). That is hotter than the surface of the sun!

The Rock Cycle

Once formed, igneous rocks do not stay the same forever. Like all other rocks, they are part of a cycle

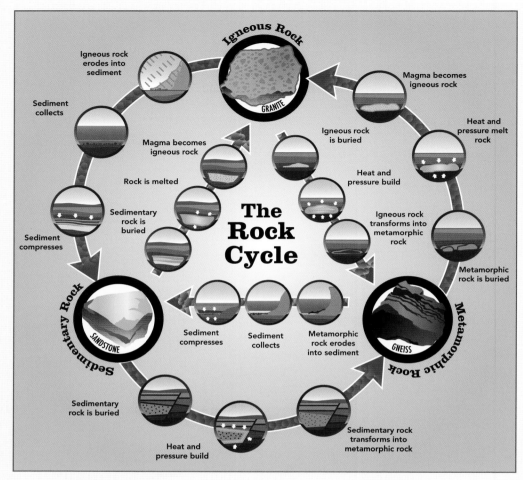

The Rock Cycle
Igneous Rock
GRANITE
Magma becomes igneous rock
Igneous rock erodes into sediment
Heat and pressure melt rock
Sediment collects
Igneous rock is buried
Magma becomes igneous rock
Heat and pressure build
Rock is melted
Igneous rock transforms into metamorphic rock
Sedimentary rock is buried
Sediment compresses
Metamorphic rock is buried
Sedimentary Rock
SANDSTONE
Sediment compresses
Sediment collects
Metamorphic rock erodes into sediment
Metamorphic Rock
GNEISS
Sedimentary rock is buried
Heat and pressure build
Sedimentary rock transforms into metamorphic rock

The Rock Cycle

This diagram shows the rock cycle. How does the information in this diagram compare to what you learned from the text about the rock cycle? What about the diagram is similar to what you read? What is different?

of change. They are formed, broken down, and

eventually recycled into new rock. This process is

called the rock cycle.

Erosion and weathering change rocks that form or are pushed above the ground. Wind and water slowly wear away bits of the rock's surface. Changes in temperature cause the rock to expand, contract—or shrink—and eventually crack. Water freezes and plants grow in the cracks, further breaking up the rock. Some of the rock's minerals dissolve in water and are washed away.

Water and wind carry the tiny broken bits of rock somewhere else. Perhaps these particles settle at the bottom of a lake to become sediment. Over millions of years, the particles are pushed closer together. New crystals may grow among them, acting like glue. The rock particles become sedimentary rock.

As sedimentary rock gets buried deeper, the heat and pressure within the earth change it into metamorphic rock. Old igneous rock can also be pressed and heated into metamorphic rock. When metamorphic rock gets hot enough, it melts. The magma from this rock makes its way toward Earth's

Erosion and weathering have formed this lone rock near Phuket Island in Thailand.

FURTHER EVIDENCE

Chapter One discusses the different types of rocks. It describes how all rocks are part of the rock cycle. What do you think is the main point of this chapter? What key evidence supports this point? Read more about how rocks change at the website below. Find a quote from the website that supports Chapter One's main point. Does the quote support an existing piece of evidence in the chapter? Or does it add a new one?

How Rocks Change
www.mycorelibrary.com/igneous-rocks

surface to form new igneous rock. Then the cycle starts again. Over time, any kind of rock can change into any other kind of rock in the rock cycle.

CHAPTER TWO

TYPES OF IGNEOUS ROCKS

All igneous rocks form from magma. But not all igneous rocks form the same way. How they form depends on the magma's journey—how and where it flows, and how close it gets to Earth's surface before it cools and hardens.

Magma is always trying to reach the surface of the earth. That is because it is less dense than the solid rock that makes up most of Earth's mantle and

Obsidian, also called volcanic glass, is an extrusive igneous rock that cools very quickly.

crust. Just as a hot-air balloon rises through cooler air, magma rises through denser rock. If conditions are right, the magma reaches the surface of the earth. Once magma reaches Earth's surface, it is called lava. It can violently erupt or gently flow from a volcano onto Earth's surface. More often, the surrounding rock is too strong for the magma to push through. The magma gets trapped below the surface. Magma that stays trapped underground forms intrusive igneous rock. Magma that reaches Earth's surface forms extrusive igneous rock.

Intrusive Rocks

Intrusive rocks are also called plutonic rocks. They are named after Pluto, the Roman god of the underworld. When magma gets trapped below the earth's surface, it takes a long time to cool. While the magma slowly cools and hardens, crystals can easily grow large enough for the naked eye to see. Sometimes they grow even bigger than you! Once the magma has

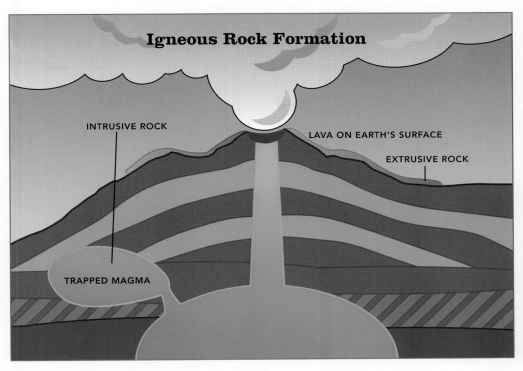

Igneous Rock Formation

Look carefully at this diagram of igneous rock formations. How does this image help you understand how igneous rocks form? Does anything look different from how you imagined it while you were reading?

cooled and hardened, the crystals cannot grow anymore. They are part of a brand-new igneous rock.

Intrusive Rock Formations

All intrusive rock formations are called plutons. Each type of pluton has a different name depending on its shape and size. Dikes are vertical sheets of rock.

The granite mountains that make up the Sierra Nevada Batholith formed underground millions of years ago.

They form when magma flows into a crack, pushing up through layers of old rock. Horizontal sheets of rock are called sills. They form when magma seeps between layers of rock. Some intrusive rock formations are massive, covering 40 square miles (100 sq km) or more. These are called batholiths. Most batholiths form beneath mountain ranges. Over time, they may become exposed through erosion. You can see one such batholith in California's Sierra Nevada.

Extrusive Rocks

Extrusive igneous rocks are also called volcanic rocks. They form from lava that spews from a volcano onto Earth's surface. When lava meets the air, it cools quickly. Minerals have little time to form crystals before the rock hardens. As a result, the crystals in extrusive rocks are usually too small to see without a microscope. Sometimes lava cools so fast that no crystals grow at all. This forms a type of rock that looks and feels like dark glass. It is called volcanic glass or obsidian.

Extrusive Rock Formations

Extrusive rocks take different forms depending on how the lava behaves. Some lava is smooth and

Volcanoes

A volcano is a pile of material that builds up around a vent, or hole, in the earth from which lava erupts. Layers of cooled lava and ash from each eruption build up around the hole. Over time, the volcano can become a tall cone or a shallow shield. Eruptions range from gentle gurgles to powerful explosions. Plinian eruptions are the most violent. Hot gases blast rock and ash miles into the sky.

19

Lava Drops

The largest rocks that form from lava drops thrown out of a volcano are called volcanic bombs. All lava drops are shaped by the wind as they cool and fall back to Earth. Sometimes the wind spins the lava into fine strands. The strands are called Pele's hair, after the Hawaiian goddess of fire and volcanoes. Many volcanoes erupt underwater. When this happens, the lava drops cool as separate clumps of rock. These lava rocks are named after their pillowy shape.

runny, like honey. As it flows down the slopes of the volcano, it forms ropelike ripples. The ripples remain in the hardened rock. Other lava is thick, like a milk shake with lots of ice cream and maybe some cookie chunks. This kind of lava is full of bits and pieces of rock. It hardens into a pile of rough rock. Another kind of lava is bubbly, like soda fizz. The bubbles leave holes in the rock, which makes it very lightweight. This kind of rock is called pumice. It forms when powerful volcanoes spew drops of lava into the air.

Harry Kaiakokonok was just six years old when he saw the Alaskan volcano Mount Katmai erupt in 1912. He later told the story of the event in an interview:

> It was just like this, bright sunshine, hot, no wind, that's when the volcano started. Started snowing like that fine pumice coming down. Make a lot of noise, the size of rice, some of it, some of it smaller, and some of it bigger, and some of it was as big as a kettle or pot . . . and pretty soon . . . dark, dark came. Dark didn't come all of a sudden, it comes gradually. Getting darker and darker and darker and darker, and pretty soon, pitch black. So black even if you put your hand two or three inches from your face outside you can't see it 'cause it was so dark.
>
> Source: Jeanne M. Schaaf. "Katmai: Witness Firsthand Accounts of the Largest Volcanic Eruption in the Twentieth Century." National Park Service. Northwind Prepress, 2004. Web. Accessed January 8, 2014.

Consider Your Audience

Read this passage carefully. Consider how you would adapt it to a different audience, such as a parent, teacher, or younger friend. Write a short essay conveying this same information to the new audience. How does your new approach differ from the original text and why?

CHAPTER THREE

IDENTIFYING IGNEOUS ROCKS

Both intrusive and extrusive igneous rocks come in a variety of colors and textures. The color of an igneous rock can tell you what minerals were in the magma it formed from. Its texture can tell you how quickly the magma cooled. With a little practice, you'll be able to tell a lot about an igneous rock just by looking at it closely.

Pumice, an extrusive rock, is easily identifiable by the holes left from bubbles in lava.

Colors and Minerals

Igneous rocks contain a few main minerals. Some may include light-colored minerals such as quartz, feldspar, and mica. They can also include dark-colored minerals such as amphibole, pyroxene, and olivine. The amount of iron in magma or a mineral determines the color. Light igneous rocks, such as pumice, have very little or no iron, while dark rocks have more iron.

You do not have to be able to recognize all of these minerals to identify igneous rocks. Scientists have come up with four categories of igneous rocks: felsic, intermediate, mafic, and ultramafic. These categories help identify igneous rocks based on their overall color.

Gems in the Rough

The mineral olivine was named for its olive-green color. Olivine gives many mafic and ultramafic igneous rocks their green hue. It is also thought to be the most common mineral in Earth's upper mantle. The most beautiful, see-through olivine crystals are cut and polished into fine gemstones. Olivine gems are called peridot.

Peridot is the gem-quality variety of the mineral olivine, which is common in mafic and ultramafic igneous rocks.

Four Categories

Felsic rocks are light in color. They might appear mostly white, beige, light gray, or pink. Felsic rocks contain lots of light-colored minerals, such as feldspar. Intermediate rocks are medium in color and are often gray. They have roughly equal amounts of light and dark minerals. Mafic rocks are dark in color. They might look gray, green, or black. Mafic rocks contain a lot of dark-colored minerals, such as olivine. Lastly, ultramafic rocks are very dark gray, green, or black. They are made up almost entirely of dark-colored minerals.

Even with these categories, color alone will not tell you everything you need to know about an igneous rock. You need a little more information before you can start labeling your rock collection. For example, two different types of rock can be the same color. One might be an intrusive rock, while the other is extrusive. How can you tell the difference?

Basic Textures

Looking at a rock's texture will help you uncover its identity. The texture of an igneous rock has to do mainly with the size of its crystals. You may remember that intrusive rocks cool slowly. This gives crystals plenty of time to grow. Extrusive rocks, on the other hand, cool quickly. Their crystals have little or no time to grow. That means intrusive rocks have larger crystals than extrusive rocks. Take a look at the igneous rock you want to identify. Can you easily see the separate crystals? If so, you have an intrusive rock. If the crystals are too small to see, it is an extrusive rock.

Intrusive rocks with large crystals are a great source for gems.

Intrusive Rock Textures

Many igneous rocks have more complex textures. For example, the crystals in some intrusive rocks can grow to enormous sizes. They can measure anywhere from one inch (2.5 cm) to several feet in length! Rocks with such giant crystals are called pegmatites. Large amounts of minerals such as mica, lithium, and tungsten can be harvested from pegmatites.

Rocks with porphyritic textures have both large and small crystals. This happens when magma begins

27

Bring On the Basalt

Basalt is the most common extrusive igneous rock on Earth. It makes up much of Earth's crust. Basalt can also be found on the surfaces of Mars and Venus as well as on the moon. Large areas of the moon are covered in basalt from long-ago lava flows. You can see these areas from Earth. Just look for the dark spots on the moon's surface. Over time, basalt sometimes forms tall columns. Tall columns of basalt can be seen in Northern Ireland at Giant's Causeway. Rapid cooling and pressure formed these columns between 50 and 60 million years ago.

to cool slowly, deep underground. Then it rises toward or onto Earth's surface, where the rest of the cooling process happens quickly. Porphyritic rocks can be either intrusive or extrusive.

Extrusive Rock Textures

Extrusive rocks have more varied textures than intrusive rocks. Some extrusive rocks have a texture similar to glass. These obsidian rocks cooled so quickly that crystals had no time to form. Obsidian has a glassy texture. It breaks into pieces with very sharp edges.

Approximately 40,000 hexagonal basalt columns make up the Giant's Causeway in Northern Ireland.

Obsidian was once highly valued for making arrowheads and other weapons and tools.

Other extrusive rocks have a spongelike texture. The hollow areas are formed by gas bubbles. You can see this texture in pumice. The hollows make pumice so lightweight that it floats on water. Pumice is often used to lighten the weight of building materials, such as concrete. Scoria is another rock with this texture. It has larger bubbles and a darker color than pumice.

Rocks with a pyroclastic texture are formed by rock and ash from an erupting volcano. They usually contain bits and pieces of rock in different sizes. Volcanic tuff is made mostly of ash. Volcanic breccia forms from larger pieces of rock, such as volcanic bombs.

EXPLORE ONLINE

The focus of Chapter Three is using color and texture to identify igneous rocks. The website below also focuses on and provides practice with identifying igneous rocks. As you know, every source is different. How is the information given in the website different from the information in this chapter? What information is the same? How do the two sources present information differently? What can you learn from this website?

Igneous Rock Identification
www.mycorelibrary.com/igneous-rocks

STUDYING IGNEOUS ROCKS

All rocks have stories to tell. Some tell us what happens deep below Earth's crust. Others tell us what happens when rocks on the surface are exposed to the sun, wind, and rain. All kinds of rock can tell geologists how the earth formed and how it is always changing. Igneous rocks are some of the most important. They make up nearly all of

Geologists learn to understand all kinds of rock, but igneous petrologists study igneous rock in particular.

Earthquakes for Science

One way geologists can find out what happens below Earth's surface is by studying earthquakes. Earthquakes produce waves of energy that travel through the inside of the planet. These waves travel at different speeds through solid rock and molten rock. By studying the waves, geologists can tell what each layer of Earth is like. They can also detect large areas of magma that might later cause volcanic eruptions.

Earth's crust. And they tell some very interesting stories.

Why Study Igneous Rocks?

People who study igneous rocks for a living are called igneous petrologists. They study the valuable information igneous rocks have to share. For example, rocks from past volcanic eruptions tell us about the volcanoes themselves. The more we understand about volcanoes, the better we can protect people from future eruptions.

Igneous rocks can also show us the best places to find important minerals. Metals such as copper, platinum, and even gold are found in and around

Geologists set up a GPS device near the volcano's center on Mount Saint Helens in 2004 to monitor earthquake activity.

igneous rocks. Large crystals can yield gems and other precious minerals. Wouldn't you like to know where to find them?

Finally, igneous rocks tell us about our planet. They provide clues to the mysteries of Earth's mantle and core. They also show how the movements of tectonic plates have shaped Earth's crust. The oldest igneous rocks can tell Earth's story almost from its beginning.

From Field to Lab

Part of an igneous petrologist's work takes place in the field. Researchers scramble over mountains and cliffs and even get close to active volcanoes. Then they record their observations of igneous rocks. They take measurements, snap photographs, and draw sketches. They also pay close attention to the surrounding rock.

After finishing their work in the field, researchers take rock samples back to the lab. Sometimes a rock's story is easy to read through its color and texture. Other times, petrologists need scientific equipment to understand an igneous rock. They use special microscopes to view crystals that are too small to see with the naked eye. Ultrathin slices of rock are glued onto glass slides. The light passing through them helps petrologists identify the minerals in the rock.

Igneous petrologists and other geologists spend much of their research time in the field, collecting and observing rocks.

The laboratory also comes in handy for studying how igneous rocks react to the heat and pressure deep inside the earth. Researchers cannot explore the earth's mantle themselves. But with high-tech equipment, they can re-create its conditions in the lab. Then they can test the igneous rock samples they gathered.

Supervolcanoes

A supervolcano is a powerful volcano that can spew rock and ash over an area of 240 cubic miles (1,000 cubic km) or more. These kinds of eruptions are more like huge explosions. And they affect the entire planet. Luckily, no supervolcano has erupted for thousands of years. Yellowstone's biggest eruption occurred more than 2 million years ago. The power of the explosion caused the volcano to collapse. The hole it left was the size of Rhode Island.

New Discoveries

Igneous petrologists have made several discoveries in recent years. Yellowstone National Park in Wyoming is home to a long-inactive supervolcano. Over the past 2 million years, it has had three giant eruptions. Scientists working in the park made a big discovery in 2013. Using earthquake data and special radar, they found that the pool of magma in the supervolcano was almost 2.5 times bigger than they had thought. It covers approximately 960 cubic miles (4,000 cubic km). The magma is well below Earth's surface for now. But no one knows when it might rise

A large pool of magma fuels Yellowstone National Park's geysers and hot springs.

and cause another massive eruption. Geologists are keeping a close eye on it.

In 2012 scientists from around the world went out to sea to investigate a deep crack in the Pacific Ocean floor. The crack, called Hess Deep, runs down to the lower part of Earth's crust. The scientists drilled into this part of the crust and took samples of the rock. The samples from Hess Deep gave geologists a clearer picture of what happens below Earth's surface.

Igneous Rocks in Space

Igneous petrologists even study rocks in space. The *Curiosity* rover sent to Mars in 2012 looks at all kinds of Martian rocks. One of the igneous rocks it came across was different from the others. It looked much more like igneous rocks found on Earth. This single rock showed that Mars might once have been very similar to the planet we live on. Scientists have also been studying rocks from Mercury. They re-created the planet's conditions in the lab. In doing so, they found that an ocean of magma might have covered Mercury billions of years ago.

Igneous rocks can tell amazing stories if you know how to read them. You don't have to be an igneous petrologist to think igneous rocks are cool. They are forming right now, somewhere beneath your feet. They are being thrown from the mouths of volcanoes. Deep in the earth, their crystals hold secrets. What will they tell you if you let them?

In 2013 scientists at the Yellowstone Volcano Observatory published an update about the hazards of Yellowstone's supervolcano:

> One should not think of Yellowstone's magma reservoir as a big cavern full of churning lava. . . . The new research shows that while the magma reservoir is bigger than we thought, the proportion of melt to solid rock . . . is similar to previous reports and appears to remain way too low for a giant eruption. . . . Scientist[s] agree that smaller eruptions are likely in the future, but the probability of ANY sort of eruption at Yellowstone still remains very low over the next 10 to 100 years.

Source: "Monitoring Upgrades Result in New Insight into Yellowstone's Magma System." USGS. US Geological Survey, December 19, 2013. Web. Accessed January 8, 2014.

What's the Big Idea?

Read this text carefully. What is the main point its author is trying to make about Yellowstone's supervolcano? Pick out a detail the author uses to make this point. What can you tell about the public's reaction to the new research in Yellowstone based on this text?

Igneous Rock Sundae

Gather chocolate chips and ice cream. Pour the chips into a saucepan. With an adult's help, melt the mixture on the stove over low heat. Stir frequently until all the chips are melted. Now you have magma! To cool your magma, carefully pour the hot mixture onto the ice cream. Wait for the magma to harden. The hardened mixture is like newly formed igneous rock. Now, dig in!

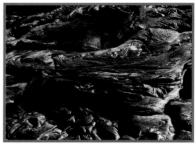

Lava cools very quickly, forming a crust, but the lava underneath can take months to cool and harden completely.

Make Your Own Volcano

For this experiment, you will need 1/3 cup of water, 4 teaspoons of baking soda, 2 teaspoons (or more) of liquid dish soap, 5 tablespoons of vinegar, red food coloring (optional), a cup, and a tray with a rim. Set your cup on a tray with a high rim. Volcanoes can be messy! First, add the water to your cup. Then mix in the baking soda and dish soap. In a separate container, measure out your vinegar. If you like, add a few drops of red food coloring to the vinegar. Now, pour the vinegar into your cup. Watch as your volcano erupts!

The drops of lava that spew from an erupting volcano can be as big as cars or small enough to float on the breeze.

Examine the size of your rocks' crystals to help you determine whether they are intrusive or extrusive.

Backyard Explorer

Grab a bag, notebook, and pencil. Then go outside to look for rocks. When you find one, write down its location. Draw a sketch of the rock in your notebook. You can even take a picture, using your hand for scale. Once you've gathered a few different rocks, it's time to head home. Examine the rocks closely. What color are they? Can you see the different minerals? How big are the crystals? How would you describe the rocks' shapes? Do they have cracks or holes? Write down your observations in your notebook. Do you think any of your rocks are igneous rocks? Why or why not?

Surprise Me

Chapter Four talks about studying igneous rocks. The field of igneous petrology can be interesting and surprising. After reading this book, what two or three facts about the study of igneous rocks did you find most surprising? Write a few sentences about each fact. Why did you find them surprising?

Why Do I Care?

Igneous rocks can be easy to overlook. But they are all around you. In what ways are igneous rocks a part of your life? How do they affect the landscape around you? Are there volcanoes near where you live? If you could get close to an active volcano, would you? If you were an igneous petrologist, what would be your favorite thing to study and why?

Say What?

Studying igneous rocks can mean learning a lot of new vocabulary. Find five words in this book that you have never seen or heard before. Use a dictionary to find out what they mean. Then write the meanings in your own words, and use each word in a new sentence.

You Are There

This book tells about the effects of living near volcanoes. Imagine that you live near a volcano. It might erupt at any time. The eruption could be harmless, or it could be deadly. Do you move away? Do you stay and see what happens? Do you explore and study the volcano? How does your family feel?

GLOSSARY

crust
Earth's rocky outer layer

erosion
the wearing away of
something by water or wind

geologist
a person who studies rocks,
soil, and land formations to
learn about Earth

igneous petrologist
a person who studies igneous
rocks

lava
hot, liquid rock that erupts
and flows onto Earth's surface

magma
hot, liquid rock found
beneath Earth's surface

mineral
a substance that is naturally
formed underground

porphyritic
a rock texture of large
crystals found in a
background of small crystals

pyroclastic
a rock texture of material that
has erupted violently from a
volcano

tectonic plate
one of several pieces of the
earth's crust that "float" on
the partially melted rock
below

weathering
to change over a long period
of time because of exposure
to sun, wind, rain, and ice

LEARN MORE

Books

Coss, Lauren. *Volcanoes.* Minneapolis: Abdo, 2013.

Dee, Willa. *Unearthing Igneous Rocks.* New York: PowerKids Press, 2014.

Tomecek, Steve. *Everything Rocks and Minerals.* Washington, DC: National Geographic, 2010.

Websites

To learn more about Rocks and Minerals, visit **booklinks.abdopublishing.com**. These links are routinely monitored and updated to provide the most current information available.

Visit **www.mycorelibrary.com** for free additional tools for teachers and students.

INDEX

ABOUT THE AUTHOR

Lisa Owings has a degree in English and creative writing from the University of Minnesota. She has written and edited a wide variety of educational books for young people. Lisa lives in Andover, Minnesota, with her husband and pets.